Original title:
The Cold Never Bothered Me…Lies

Copyright © 2024 Creative Arts Management OÜ
All rights reserved.

Author: Finn Donovan
ISBN HARDBACK: 978-9916-94-264-2
ISBN PAPERBACK: 978-9916-94-265-9

When Warmth is a Mirage

In sunshine's glow, I wear my coat,
A heatwave dream, who needs a boat?
I sip my cocoa, sweat drips down,
While folks around me wear a frown.

The sun's a trick, a playful jest,
I'm in my parka, feeling blessed.
With mittens on, I dance and twirl,
While summer's promise starts to whirl.

Silent Storms of Deceit

A snowflake lands upon my nose,
Whispers sweet nothings as it goes.
I know in secret, warmth is fake,
That winter's bite is all at stake.

With boots so tall, my feet are warm,
While inner thoughts begin to swarm.
The chill I greet with laughter loud,
Yet freeze beneath my fluffy shroud.

Winter's False Embrace

In frosty nights, we laugh and cheer,
A hug from winter, we all fear.
With each soft flake, I feel the tease,
The kind of love that stings like freeze.

A jacket thick, I shuffle slow,
As frosty winds begin to blow.
Yet in this chill, I find delight,
With snowball fights that last all night.

Subzero Secrets

Under blankets, secrets thaw,
Chilled hearts masked by winter's law.
With cheeky grins, we sip hot tea,
For warmth is where the laughter be.

The icy air can't steal our cheer,
With cozy socks, we persevere.
We share our tales of frosty plight,
While making snowmen in twilight.

Chill in the Silence

In frosty air, my breath is white,
I laugh and play, it feels so right.
But wait, what's that? A shiver shoots,
A hidden truth, in winter's boots.

The snowflakes dance, they tickle my nose,
Yet I deny how much it froze.
A frozen grin, a cheeky glance,
I fake the heat, just join the dance.

Frosted Facades

The chill invites a merry cheer,
I'll claim it's fun, let's have a beer!
But as I sip, my fingers freeze,
I'm acting bold, but really wheeze.

My jacket's thick, I strut with pride,
Yet shivers sneak where I can't hide.
Oh look, a laugh, a cozy tale,
While winter whispers, cold and pale.

Beneath the Frozen Mask

With rosy cheeks, I boast I'm fine,
My grin is wide, but inside I pine.
A snowman waves, he sees my plight,
While I'm inside, a frozen fright.

I tell tall tales of winter's glee,
But can't deny what's chilling me.
Beneath the mask, the truth is smooth,
A chilly heart, in need of soothe.

Icy Whispers in the Wind

Here comes the breeze, it makes me sway,
I laugh aloud, I'll be okay!
Yet down inside, there's truth untold,
For icy bites can chill the bold.

A winter night, so clear, so bright,
But cloaked in frost, it's all a fright.
I twirl and spin, pretend I'm grand,
But blizzards freeze my funny hand.

The Glacial Illusion

It's freezing out, but I'm quite fine,
A frosty vibe, I'm on cloud nine.
With every shiver, a chuckle escapes,
In this winter wonderland, I take my shapes.

But oh, the truth hides under ice,
My rosy cheeks aren't quite so nice.
As snowflakes dance upon my nose,
I smile wide as the winter blows.

Embracing the Frosted Facade

I strut in shorts, a frosty king,
With my shades on, I feel the spring.
Each penguin glance makes me feel bold,
While my toes shiver, my story's told.

I hold my mug like a trophy high,
Claiming warmth from the hot cocoa pie.
But under the layers, I secretly cringe,
As the frostbite threatens to unhinge.

Beneath the Ice, a Flame

Beneath the frost, my warmth resides,
In wooly socks, my humor hides.
With every slip and playful fall,
I laugh it off – I've got it all.

Ice castles gleam with artful grace,
While I'm just trying to keep my pace.
But listen closely, you might hear,
My frozen thoughts all loud and clear.

Surfaces Like Glass

The sidewalk glimmers, oh what a charm,
I walk like a dancer, with laughter to warm.
Yet beneath my bravado, a secret I keep,
That icy patch has me counting my sheep.

With every slip, my ego takes flight,
I'm the star of the show in this winter night.
So let them laugh at my glorious fall,
For in this chill, I will have a ball.

Secrets Behind the Winter Veil

Snowflakes fall, I must confess,
Winter's charm, what a mess!
Hot cocoa's just a trick, you see,
It's really all just fantasy.

Hats and scarves, for fashion's sake,
Underneath, I start to shake.
Frosty winds, a tickle to my nose,
Oh, how I wish for summer's clothes!

January's Untruths

January's bright, or so they say,
But my toes freeze every day.
They claim it's fun to make snowmen,
But I've lost fingers now and then.

Ice cream sundaes feel so right,
'Til they chill me every night.
Warm boots are just a clever ploy,
To hide the cold from all your joy!

In the Shadow of the Icicle

Icicles dangle, sharp and mean,
A winter's joke or something unseen?
They twinkle bright, but oh so sly,
Just waiting for a passerby.

Snowball fights, they seem so fun,
'Til you're hit and start to run.
Laughter rings beneath the frost,
But tell me, who's the real boss?

Cool Comforts and Chilled Confessions

Hot soup warms, or so they claim,
But my lips freeze, this ain't no game!
They serve it with a smile so wide,
While I'm shivering, trying to hide.

Cozy blankets, soft and thick,
Yet somehow they still feel like brick.
Bring on the sun, I need a tan,
This frosty myth is part of the plan!

Layers of Ice Overlying Whispers

Snowflakes dance with light and cheer,
Under the chill, I persevere.
But shivers writhe beneath my grin,
A frosty tale; where do I begin?

Warm thoughts bubble, I play the game,
Wiggle my toes, but not quite the same.
Sipping tea with shivers so sly,
Wrapped in warmth, yet I cannot lie.

Each chilly breeze tickles my skin,
Pretending it's all a joyful spin.
Winter shadows laugh at my guise,
While I just nod and share my cries.

So here I stand, a snowman's twin,
A frosty joke beneath this skin.
With layers thick, I still feel bright,
In a winter's laugh, I find delight.

Frozen Facade of Crystal Lies

Frosty mornings bring out my grin,
With a face that sparkles, the chill begins.
I plaster smiles on this frozen frame,
Pretending warmth is just the same.

Sipping cocoa that's more like ice,
Sugar-coated lies, oh so nice!
Wrapped in layers, oh what a hoot,
In a world of frost, my boots salute.

I build a fortress of frozen wit,
Where laughter echoes but never quite fit.
With every slip on the icy floor,
I chuckle lightly, who could ask for more?

So here I stand, the queen of cold,
In my crystal lies, so bright and bold.
While winter's breath refuses to cease,
I take a bow, all wrapped in fleece.

Winter's Mask of Hidden Truths

Checkered mittens, such playful guise,
Hiding warmth in winter's lies.
Each snowball tossed is a well-honed jest,
While inside, I'm cozy, rigidness expressed.

With each frosty wind that I chase,
I giggle softly at my frozen face.
Snowy cheeks hide a silent sigh,
But I'll pretend as the snowflakes fly.

My laugh's a blanket, soft yet cold,
Beneath the mask, stories unfold.
Sliding on ice, what wonderful fun,
In a world of chill, I'm never done.

So come join me in this winter show,
Where the mask of truth puts on quite a glow.
With every slip and every sight,
I burst with laughter, a frozen delight.

Frosted Echoes of a Warm Heart

In the brisk breeze, my heart does mock,
Chipper and bright despite the clock.
I wear a parka though I'm quite warm,
Wrapped in laughter, avoiding the swarm.

Chatter of frost like sweet little lies,
Pretend to shiver 'neath gray winter skies.
I bounce through flurries, no worries I keep,
For inside this heart, it's a warm little beep.

But each winter night, when silence holds tight,
I chuckle at comedy, lost in the night.
Slipping and sliding, making my mark,
In an icy world, I light up the dark.

So join me, friend, in this chilly ballet,
With frosted echoes, we'll dance and sway.
In layers so thick, we'll giggle and prance,
Deceiving the frost with a warm-hearted dance.

Illusions in the Winter Glow

Snowflakes dance like little stars,
While I sip cocoa from a jar.
Laughing at the frosty breeze,
But inside, I crave the heat, not freeze.

Hats and mittens all around,
Yet warmth is nowhere to be found.
Outside smiles, a chill inside,
Oh, how I wish it was bright and wide.

Ice on windows, a frosty show,
Pretending I'm a winter pro.
But in my heart, I truly know,
I long for sun, not ice and snow.

So here I am in winter's light,
Joking hard, though not quite right.
With dreams of beaches in my head,
Wishing for a warm slice of bread.

A Chill in the Air of Pretenses

Fluffy coats and hats so grand,
But inside, I'm like a frozen strand.
I prance around, oh what a show,
While deep down, I miss the glow.

Hot cocoa spills, laughter spills too,
Who knew winter's laugh could feel so blue?
Frosty bites touch cheeks with glee,
But inside my warmth is a distant plea.

Snowball fights and silly pranks,
Meanwhile, I'm daydreaming of sandy banks.
All this cold, it's quite a jest,
Yet my heart yearns for summer's rest.

We jump and shout, we sing and freeze,
Yet dreaming of a summer breeze.
A chill indeed, but it's all so fun,
In this winter's game, we're never done!

Lies Wrapped in a Snowball

Little frost, a dazzling guise,
Hiding truth beneath the skies.
Snowballs fly as laughter rings,
But inside, my heart just stings.

I'm bundled up, a festive sight,
Pretending all is warm and bright.
But layers thick can't hide the freeze,
While I make snowmen with such ease.

Crisp air nips and giggles swell,
I toss a ball, all's well, I tell.
But frosty fingers and frozen toes,
Reveal the truths that winter shows.

So here I am, acting tough,
Wishing inside for warmth enough.
With every flake, my secret kept,
The sun is what my heart adept!

Cloaked in Winter's Deceit

Icicles hang, a lovely sight,
Yet shiver threatens to ignite.
I dance in snow with festive cheer,
While truth in layers hides, I fear.

Mittens warm, but fingers numb,
In this cold, my smile's a hum.
Jokes are cracked, laughter flows,
But underneath, a cold heart grows.

Gloves and boots, a fashion state,
But where's the warmth, oh isn't it great?
Feigning joy in winter's bite,
While dreaming of a sunlight flight.

So here I plight, draped in white,
Spinning tales in the frosty night.
All these jokes and playful schemes,
Mask the chill of winter's dreams.

The Embrace of Shattered Icy Truths

I wore shorts when snowflakes danced,
And claimed I thrived in winter's trance.
My teeth chattered in a noble pose,
While dreams of sunbeams nobody knows.

The wind howled jokes, I laughed too loud,
In frosty air, I felt quite proud.
I stomped and stumbled on my way,
Pretending ice wouldn't make me sway.

Hot cocoa's warmth was just a show,
As frozen fingers made me glow.
With every slip, I'd burst with glee,
'Twas just a game—so funny to me!

So here's to winter's chilly jest,
With shivering bodies, we are blessed.
In laughter's warmth, we'll surely find,
The joy that lies in icy grind.

Warming Up to the Winter's Facade

I donned my mittens made of fluff,
Pretended they were warm enough.
In every snowball fight so grand,
I bragged about my frosty stand.

Sipping tea that steamed and swirled,
I told tall tales of this cold world.
"My heart beats strong in frozen air!"
While numbness crept—I hardly cared.

Each gust of wind became a friend,
Said, "Oh, I love how cold can bend!"
But in my socks, my toes turned blue,
Still claiming gems in icy dew.

Beneath it all, I felt the chill,
With every laugh, it added thrill.
So here's the truth, a frosty dare—
I'd trade for sun with nary a care!

Frozen Lies Under the Northern Lights

Under the lights, the stories spun,
Of daring feats on ice, oh what fun!
I skated 'round with grace and flair,
While secretly, I gripped the air.

With every slip, I roared with glee,
"Oh look at me, the mighty bee!"
Yet, landing soft, my heart did quake,
In frozen truth, I'd start to shake.

The chilling winds, I laughed and cackled,
As icy slips made my knees crackle.
With every fall, I'd claim my prize,
The giggles hid the frosty lies.

Among the stars, my heart took flight,
In frozen tales beneath the night.
But deep inside, I knew the ruse,
The truth was cold, yet made me muse.

Beneath the Surface of Frigid Dreams

Beneath the snow, where secrets dwell,
I strutted proud like a winter spell.
With every frost, I told myself,
That I could be a stealthy elf.

In layers thick, I wore my pride,
But in my heart, the warmth would hide.
Each slip on ice—a comedic show,
Where jokes ran wild in the freezing flow.

I shouted tales of winter cheer,
While sipping tea to fight my fear.
But under frosted smiles and cheer,
Lay heated thoughts of summer near.

So let the snowflakes softly fall,
In this frosty game, I'll take it all.
With laughter's light, I'll brave the chill,
For humor warms the winter's thrill.

Echoes of a Frigid Heart

In a world so numb and gray,
Where snowflakes dance in disarray,
I claim I'm fine, a frosty cheer,
But my teeth chatter; that's the fear.

With mittens thick and scarf well-tied,
I strut along with frosty pride,
Yet underneath this frozen guise,
I moan and groan with icy sighs.

I'll build a snowman, wide and tall,
He'll have a grin, won't care at all,
Yet deep inside this winter's bite,
I'm lost in shivers, not delight.

So here's to laughter, cold as ice,
With every joke, I pay the price,
For I can't wait until it's spring,
And out of hibernation, I will spring!

Deceptive Gleam of Ice

A twinkling frost upon the grass,
Oh, how I love the winter class!
I skip and leap with joyful glee,
Whilst secretly, I want some tea.

The sun shines through the icy veil,
As I pretend with a big exhale,
But every snowdrift's got a tale,
Of frozen toes and heavy flail.

My hat's adorned with flurries white,
Like I'm the queen of winter's night,
But underneath the cozy gear,
I'm shivering, despite the cheer.

I laugh and play in this white zone,
Wishing for the heat, just let it be known,
The icy twinkle can't deceive,
If only warmth could make me believe!

Lying in the Frost

Laying on the crunchy snow,
I tell myself, 'This is the show,'
With all my friends, I smile so bright,
    While wishing for a firelight.

Snow angels flapping, freezing bliss,
I shout, 'Oh yes!' but feel remiss,
Though winter's charm is quite a jest,
    Underneath, I crave a rest.

With frozen fingers, I take that plunge,
Into the snow, I'm free to lunge,
But deep inside, my heart does plead,
For cozy blankets; that's my need.

So as we roll and laugh and play,
My body's whining every way,
Give me a sunlit, warm embrace,
And let me leave this icy place!

Snowflakes' Hidden Stories

Each flake that falls, a frosty jest,
Whispers, 'You love this, do your best!'
I nod along, pretend it's grand,
While clutching tight my icy hand.

A winter wonderland of cheer,
Yet inside me, I grumble, dear,
I keep on smiling, all a show,
As bitter winds begin to blow.

I sip my cocoa with a grin,
While hoping spring will soon begin,
The world is white, it sparkles bright,
But all I want is warmth at night.

So here's to snow, with all its flair,
And frosty air; I'll make a dare,
To laugh and dance, pretend to thaw,
While hiding from the chill's cruel claw!

The Arctic Veil of Deception

In jackets thick, we strut with pride,
Beneath the fluff, our chill we hide.
Sipping cocoa, smiles so wide,
Yet under layers, shivers abide.

Snowflakes dance, so light and free,
While clutching hot hands, that's the key.
We freeze our toes in winter's spree,
But laugh it off, oh can't you see?

Igloos built with sheer delight,
As hearts race fast through frosty night.
But chill creeps in, a sneaky plight,
And we pretend all's sunny bright.

Whispers float like snowy dreams,
In winter's grip, we twist and scheme.
Wrapped up tight, we stifle screams,
Oh, it's all part of our grand theme.

Serpents of Ice and Warm Dreams

A snake of frost wraps 'round my feet,
Yet on this ice, I dance, so fleet.
With dreams of warmth, I still compete,
While frozen toes can't take the heat.

Skiing down with joyful glee,
Pretending we're as bold as can be.
But snowballs fly, oh woe is me,
For all my bravado's just not free.

Winter's serpent, sly and lean,
Serpentine moves, oh what a scene!
We grin through chills, a cheerful glean,
'Cause cozy thoughts are truly keen.

In frosty air, we're wrapped in laughter,
Chasing dreams that come after.
And though it's cold, we're madly dafter,
Playing games, a winter's rafter.

Treading upon the Frost of Frailty

Upon the frost, I take a stride,
With fluffy socks, I swell with pride.
Yet underneath, I cannot hide,
The little shivers that coincide.

With laughter loud, we skitter fast,
Pretending autumn's here to last.
But frosted noses, they contrast,
And warmth is something we all cast.

As ice turns soft beneath our weight,
We trip and stumble, oh the fate!
With all this fun, we still await,
A brief reprieve, don't hesitate!

We sip and munch by fireside glow,
Denial's game, we play it slow.
Through tangled yarn and winter's show,
We find our cheer, then melt the snow.

The Lie Beneath Winter's Gaze

Under the guise of frosty stars,
We claim we're tough, oh look at scars!
With smiles bright and winter jars,
Yet shivering hearts hide their memoirs.

The snowflakes fall, in jackets cocooned,
Warmth declared, but truth festooned.
Beneath the laughter, the truth's marooned,
While chilly winds by jokes are tuned.

In winter's grip, we dance about,
But deep inside, there lurks a doubt.
With playful nudges, we're left without,
The warmth we crave, so stick it out!

So raise a glass to frosty fun,
With winter's tales, we laugh and run.
For in the cold, we all are one,
Our frosty lies, a chill undone.

Embracing the Chill of Untruths

I bundled up in tales so bright,
A cloak of fibs in winter's night.
They whispered sweet, a frosty charm,
Yet underneath, there's little harm.

With every jest, I laugh and play,
As ice cubes dance, they tease and sway.
In this grand freeze of made-up cheer,
Who knew a fib could warm so near?

Promises like snowflakes fall,
Melt away, we'll laugh them all.
In frozen truth, we weave a quilt,
Of warmth from every tale we built.

So here's to lies in winter's grip,
They make us smile, and that's the trip!
With frosty breaths, our giggles rise,
It's all in jest, beneath the skies.

Snowflakes and Secrets

Snowflakes swirl, like whispers low,
Each one hides a secret glow.
Wrapped in layers, giggles spread,
A frosty story, lightly tread.

Watch the wonders, lies take flight,
Like snowmen built on winter's night.
With carrots for noses, checks so bright,
But melting truths fade out of sight.

Giggles echo through the chill,
As snowy scenes the heart can fill.
These frigid tales we spin so light,
Keep warm our souls, till dawn's first light.

In fluffy mounds of white and gray,
Lies dance 'round, and we will play.
With each snowflake, joy will rise,
In this chilly world of sunny lies.

The Bitter Taste of Chilly Denials

With each denial, a frosty bite,
A chilly twist, oh what a sight!
Wrapped in claims, we stroll so bold,
In winter slippers, hearts never cold.

"What? Me lie?" with a wink I say,
As snowmen nod and children play.
I sip hot cocoa, laughter warm,
While frigid truths flee from the swarm.

With every gulp, the truth may sting,
But who cares when snowflakes sing?
In this cozy world of wintry spice,
Denials taste like sugar and ice.

So give a cheer for frosty cheer,
For chilly tales we hold so dear.
In each bitter twist, we find delight,
In playful jests, the world feels right.

Frosty Veils of Comfort

Beneath the frost, a cozy veil,
Wrapped in comfort, we regale.
With every breath, a laugh escapes,
In chilly smiles, we tease in shapes.

Frosty nights bring tales anew,
Lies like snowflakes, fresh and true.
Grinning wide, we strut in glee,
In this frozen maze of jubilee.

So gather 'round the warming fire,
With frosty lies that don't expire.
In laughter's heat, the cold retreats,
We dance and jig on snowy streets.

Embrace the chill with silly cheer,
For frosty veils bring loved ones near.
With every fib, a warmth we share,
In winter's grasp, we show we care.

Beneath the Rime of Falsehood

In a world of ice so slick,
I claim it's nice, just a little trick.
Snowflakes tickle with icy hands,
While I pretend to make grand plans.

Frosty cheeks and a frozen nose,
But inside, the heat of laughter glows.
Laughing with mittens and goofy grins,
Embracing the chill with faux chagrins.

A nod to winter's frigid breeze,
As I sip cocoa with joyful ease.
With every gulp, I shiver and shake,
While faking warmth, for goodness' sake!

So raise your mugs to winter's chill,
As we dance and sing against our will.
Behind the jokes and frosty cheer,
Lies a heart that's never near.

Frosty Masks in a Warm World

A winter wonderland, so bright and bold,
But I'm wrapped up in stories untold.
With frosty masks that hide my face,
I laugh at cold in this cozy place.

Snowball fights with a cheeky grin,
But inside, the heat is wearing thin.
Huddled close to the fire's glow,
While jesting the frost, I steal a show.

Each icy breath, a puff of air,
Faking bravery as I pretend to care.
But underneath this joking guise,
The winter's chill is no sweet surprise.

So let's toast to this frosty spree,
Embracing the snowflakes, irony!
With every giggle and clumsy slide,
The warmth we seek is just a ride.

Veils of the Arctic Mind

Wrapped in scarves that swallow whole,
I strut like a penguin, oh what a role!
With frosty glares and silly hats,
I make light of what life hands - spats!

Under the chill, my giggles stir,
As I toss snow like a fuzzy blur.
But when the freeze bites down deep,
My warm thoughts flee, like a dreamer's leap.

Slipping on ice, I make my case,
While faking poise, I lose my grace.
Yet everyone smiles, it's quite the sight,
In a dance that spins through the frosty night.

So I pile on layers, thick and wide,
Pretending I glide while I truly slide.
With laughter ringing, the truth's in sight,
That winter's a jest, even if it bites.

Deceit Wrapped in a Winter's Embrace

In this frosty world, I strut and prance,
With a grin that's wide, I take my chance.
Pretending to revel in icy bliss,
While secretly hoping for warm, sweet kiss.

Snowmen crafted with too much flair,
In a landscape that says, 'I'm just not there!'
With funny hats and carrot noses,
Poking fun, as the winter dozes.

Each icicle hanging is a trick to play,
While my heart craves a sunlit day.
But here I am, in a frozen jest,
Doing my best to brave the quest.

So let them laugh at my frosty fight,
As I claim the cold feels just so right.
Wrapped in layers and warm-hearted cheer,
I dance through winter, with grins from ear to ear.

Frostbitten Dreams of Authenticity

In winter's grasp, we joke and play,
As frozen figures dance away.
We shiver, laugh, and mock the chill,
Wrapped in layers, we've lost our will.

A frosty breeze, we raise a cheer,
What's icy here brings warmth, oh dear!
With snowball fights and laughter bright,
Who needs the sun? This feels just right!

The snowmen grin with noses bright,
Their carrot smiles a frosty sight.
We boast of warmth, but feel the freeze,
Wrapped in down, our hearts at ease.

So here we sip hot cocoa warm,
In dreams of summer, we find our charm.
The ice may bite, but who would care?
In this frosty land, we shed our despair.

Hushed Lies in the Glacial Silence

Whispers float on chilling air,
Smiles frozen, do we even care?
We waddle forth in puffy coats,
In hushed tones, we share our quotes.

The winds may howl, the snowflakes quake,
Yet here we are, for laughter's sake.
Under clouds, we boldly prance,
With cheeks so red, we risk a chance.

In blizzards fierce, we tell our tales,
Of steamy nights and sunlit sails.
But truth be told, we'd choose the chill,
For snowball fights bring quite the thrill!

So let the frost do what it may,
We'll sip our drinks in frosty play.
With laughter ringing through the night,
We'll dance on ice, and shine so bright.

Fables Beneath the Icy Canopy

Beneath a sky of wintry gray,
We craft our fables, come what may.
With rosy cheeks and noses red,
We spin our tales while dreams are fed.

In snowy realms, we boldly speak,
Of summers past and days unique.
Though frost may bite and winter tease,
We find our fun with perfect ease.

The pine trees sway in icy dance,
Each flake a whimsy, a playful chance.
In laughter's realm, we stake our claim,
As winter dresses us in fame.

So gather 'round, you frosty friends,
Our tales will weave until the end.
In icy laughter, we will shine,
For in this frigid world, we're fine.

Glaciers of Truth in a Sea of White

In a sea of white, we drift and glide,
With winter's charm, we take it in stride.
The glaciers form with secrets kept,
In frozen depths, our stories swept.

We joke of warmth 'neath icy skies,
With shivers masked as silly lies.
The world is crisp, we joke and tease,
As laughter whispers in the breeze.

A snowman's hat, a crooked grin,
We build our dreams, let laughter win.
In frosted realms, we find our place,
With cheerful hearts and frozen grace.

So let the winds of winter blow,
We'll dance along, with a merry show.
With joy and fun in every plight,
In shimmering snow, we find our light.

Icy Winds Carrying Distant Truths

A frosty breeze whispers sweet designs,
It tells of snowmen who sip like wines.
With mittens on hands, we proudly strut,
While shaking in boots, oh what a cut!

With smiles like icicles on faces wide,
We claim it's a blast, no need to hide.
But teeth start to chatter, each breath a puff,
How funny, this winter? Quite a bluff!

Snowflakes are falling, like confetti in June,
We dance through the madness, a frosty cartoon.
Riding on sleds like we own the whole place,
But warmth's the true king, can't keep up the pace!

So cheers to the chill, raise a glass of ice,
To shivering laughter, it's almost nice.
We'll laugh off the freeze, and play with the frost,
For deep in the cold, it's our warmth that's lost!

Treading on the Edge of Frosted Reality

Walking on pathways of glistening white,
We trip on our laughter, what a silly sight.
With slip-and-slide shoes, we bob and we weave,
Who knew it was hard just to try and believe?

Chattering teeth while we're claiming it's fun,
Freezing in laughter 'til the day is done.
The wind whispers secrets, all icy and bright,
Yet here we are, bundled up tight!

As snowmen take over our yard with their glee,
We wave at the mailman, all jolly and free.
Our noses turn red, like a deer in the headlight,
With tales of the frost, it's a frosty delight!

So here's to the chill, like a wintery jest,
Each frostbitten smile, we truly are blessed.
With mittens and boots, we dance through the haze,
In this frosted reality, we find our own ways!

Unmasking the Winter's Grit

Peering out windows at the snowflakes that fall,
We're cozy inside, but hear their harsh call.
With cocoa in hand, we pretend we're fierce,
Yet outside lies a blizzard that makes us all pierce!

In layers of sweaters, we think we're so sly,
While penguins laugh hard as we tumble and fly.
Our shovels are weapons, we wield with great flair,
Yet all that we want is just warmth and good air!

We puff out our chests as we brave the deep drifts,
Yet dread every flake like we're unwrapping gifts.
With each hardy stomp, our bravado starts to freeze,
Guess winter's no joke, it's a slippery tease!

So let's raise a cheer for the laughter we share,
In the face of the frost, we're still hanging there.
Gritting our teeth, gripping hard on our hats,
Unmasking the winter while we fall like old cats!

Harsh Mornings of Deceptive Sunlight

The sun peeks through my window bright,
Bringing cheer with morning light.
Yet my bed, it begs me to stay,
In dreams where warmth does play.

With coffee strong, I greet the day,
But chilly drafts just won't obey.
A sweater on, I start to shiver,
Why's life a constant game of sliver?

The birds are chirping, "What a treat!"
But outside, it's more like frozen feet.
I laugh and grin, pretend it's nice,
While secretly wishing for a warm slice.

The thermostat lies high and proud,
But I'm wrapped up, under a cloud.
Bright sunlight's a crafty jest,
In its glow, I never feel blessed.

Heartstrings Entwined in Frost

They say love's warm, a cozy spark,
But frigid winds leave quite a mark.
Wrapped in layers, this dance of hearts,
Feels like winter with all its parts.

Whispers of sweet nothings unfold,
While icicles hang, silent and cold.
A hug from you, I might comply,
But not if snowflakes start to fly.

Sledding down this snowy hill,
With heartstrings pulled, it's quite the thrill.
Yet every cuddle, every kiss,
Comes with a frostbite kind of risk.

So let's toast with hot cocoa delight,
Laughing in this frosty night.
For love in winter, let's just pretend,
That frozen hearts can still ascend.

Whispering Winds of Disguised Truths

The wind is howling, or is it talking?
Promises made, but I'm just squawking.
It tells me tales of warmer days,
While I'm bundled up in a cold malaise.

Each rustle of leaves, a sneaky ploy,
Wrapping me up in a tricky joy.
"I'm fine! I swear! Just feeling bright!"
While my nose is red, what a silly sight!

I take a step, the ice gives way,
Laughing loudly at my ballet.
The humor in slipping, it's all a game,
With "I meant to fall!" playing all the same.

So here's to gusts that tickle and tease,
To half-truths spoken by chilly breeze.
In this comedy, I'll wear my grin,
Though inside I'm shivering; let the fun begin!

Chilling Echoes of Past Lies

Once I believed, 'It'll be just fine,'
But winter laughed, said, "You'll dine."
On chilly air and frosty flakes,
A banquet served with silly mistakes.

Echoes of warmth linger in dreams,
But reality's cruel with icy beams.
I laugh at the past's quick deceit,
Like finding cold peas in my winter treat.

Remembering times when we sat by the fire,
All cozy and warm, with comfort to admire.
Now I grab blankets and sip on my tea,
Wishing those sweet days would come back to me.

Yet here I stand, a smile on my face,
In this frosty realm, I embrace the space.
For every chill carries humor, it seems,
In winter's arms, I'll dance with my dreams.

Glacial Grins

In snowflake smiles, we dance around,
Telling tales of warmth, oh what a sound!
With every shiver, we crack a joke,
As ice wraps tightly, the laughter's no hoax.

Frosted fingers wave in delight,
Pretending the chill feels just right.
Hot cocoa stories, we sip with glee,
But underneath that mug, it's just not to be.

In fluffy boots, we stomp and play,
While frozen thoughts start to sway.
Chattering teeth, a comedy show,
Yet inside, we're longing for sun's warm glow.

So join this party of chilly reprieve,
With frosty jokes, we'll never leave.
The grin stays wide, a mask we wear,
As winter whispers, "Do you really care?"

Frigid Facets of Truth

A snowman's smile, a complex sight,
Beneath that façade, it's not quite right.
We claim to love the winter's charm,
As toes go numb, what a false alarm!

Each breath a cloud in the frosty air,
"I thrive in ice," we loudly declare.
But shivers sneak in, oh what a gaffe,
As we snicker quietly, trying to laugh.

The icy jokes hang like stalactites,
In the glow of bulbs, we find our fights.
Pretending it's fab to freeze and bite,
While wishing for warmth on a winter's night.

Come forth, dear friends, in layers dense,
We'll share our truths, with some pretence.
As the frost creeps in, with smiles we cheer,
Unraveling warmth in the chill we fear.

Breath of the Betrayed

A puff of air becomes a lie,
As frosty whispers float up to the sky.
"I love this chill," we boldly state,
While secretly dreaming of a warm plate.

With each frosted step, we laugh and slip,
Telling ourselves we love this trip.
But in the silence, our socks grow wet,
A winter surprise we won't soon forget.

Like penguins waddling in search of heat,
We shuffle around on our snowy feet.
"I'll take the cold," our voices sing,
As hidden beneath is a longing thing.

So gather close, beneath the freeze,
Let's toast to fun, to laughter, to tease.
For in this frost, our spirits will sway,
Though in the back, we wish for May.

Frost-Kissed Facades

With rosy cheeks, we venture out,
In winter's clutch, we scream and shout.
"I'm loving this snow," we can't help but cheer,
While inside we're cold, that's perfectly clear.

As spitting sleet blurs our sunny hopes,
We jingle our keys, adorned like dopes.
Muffled giggles hide in puffy coats,
While we clink our mugs like eager goats.

The wind laughs back as we try to flee,
From icy talons, oh woe is me!
"Let's build a fort," we connive in jest,
But all we want is a cozy nest.

So come, fellow dreamers, join this dance,
Under frosty skies, take a chance.
For in the gleam of shimmering frost,
Lies laughter's warmth, despite what's lost.

Beneath the Frosty Veil of Deceit

Underneath this chilly guise,
Lies a warmth in my blue skies.
Icicles dangle from the eaves,
Yet I can't help but laugh and tease.

Snowflakes dance in merry jest,
Claiming winter is the best.
With mittens stuffed, I'm feeling brave,
But frozen toes? I'm not a knave!

Frosty breath, I make a show,
Sipping cocoa, oh so slow.
Pretending chill's my favorite friend,
While secretly, I just pretend.

Under layers, I hide my glee,
Waltzing 'round with icy glee.
Smiles masked by winter's bite,
In this frosted play, all is bright.

The Ice that Shields the Heart

I've wrapped my soul in ice so clear,
Hoping you won't come too near.
Chilling tales I like to spin,
While secretly, I'm warm within.

With every frostbite, I delight,
Claiming I'll snowball you tonight.
But underneath that winter frown,
Lies a heart that won't back down.

It's a slippery slope, this frosty game,
Exaggerated tales, oh what a shame!
Yet still I trot through winter's breeze,
Warmed by laughter, trying to please.

So many jokes on ice, you see,
Each one a flake of pure esprit.
I'll laugh and jest while feeling bold,
In this winter tale, the truth is cold.

Frigid Smiles, Warm Intentions

On a snowy hill, I fake a grin,
While wishing for sunshine to begin.
With frosty cheeks, the fun's still there,
Underlying warmth shows I care.

Wrapped in layers, a comedic sight,
I tumble down with all my might.
Winter's charm? A playful ruse,
Embarking on this chilly cruise.

Hot cocoa smiles cover my face,
Pretending I'm not in this cold race.
From frozen lips, the laughter flows,
In this winter tale, everyone knows.

Gloves and scarves hide vibrant hues,
That burst forth when the sun breaks through.
But until then, in snow I lie,
Warming hearts while pretending to cry.

Illusions of Warmth Amidst the Frost

Oh, look at me in my winter wear,
With a brave facade, I manage to dare.
Telling stories of icy thrills,
While running with those vibrant chills.

Mirage of warmth in a frozen zone,
Where laughter echoes in the cold alone.
With blanket forts and snowball fights,
I jest about the frigid nights.

I'll build a fire with laughter light,
While shivering under the moon's bright light.
Claiming romance in icy hearts,
But truth be told, it's just for laughs.

So here's to winter's silly game,
In stark contrast to the sun's great fame.
Behind the frost, where giggles play,
I'll find my warmth in a funny way.

Clarion Calls in the Winter Silence

Snowflakes tumble, what a show,
I'm bundled up, but still feel faux.
The winds do whistle, quite the scream,
Yet here I stand, all cozy, dream.

Frosty fingers knock on doors,
I smile and sip my cocoa pours.
A frozen mouth, I try to cheer,
Pretending I have naught to fear.

The ice outside is slick and fresh,
But in my heart, I feel the mesh.
Like penguins brave, I waddle forth,
With laughter stifled, but of worth.

So here I jest, while snowflakes fall,
In winter's grip, I find my call.
Though chattering teeth play their game,
Inside I'm laughing, all the same.

The Dance of Ice and Hidden Flames

Outside it's icy, don't you know,
While here I dance, with fire's glow.
I shimmy past the chilling breeze,
  In fuzzy socks, I do as I please.

Icicles dangle, sharp and bright,
Yet I shun them, it's sheer delight.
With every slip, I twirl and spin,
  Pretend I'm graceful, with a grin.

Underneath my scarf, I chuckle low,
As carolers freeze and catch the show.
I'm a winter queen in a heated land,
  With tea and jokes all close at hand.

So laugh I will, in snowy style,
For under layers, I'll beguile.
With every frosty step I take,
  Winter's mirth, I shall awake.

Discordant Chords of a Frozen Melody

A symphony of crunching feet,
As snow begrudgingly meets the street.
I sing a tune in muffled tones,
Where laughter swirls with ice and stones.

Carrots for noses, a snowman's frown,
I pose right next to him in gown.
He may be frosty, stiff, and white,
But here I am, ready to ignite.

With snowballs packed, I launch a throw,
And dodge the flake-filled undertow.
In this chilly, wild charade,
I'm stirring chaos as I parade.

Mismatched socks and frozen toes,
Yet still I dance, despite the woes.
A silly tune in winter's plight,
I'll take this stage, my joy ignites.

Crystalline Lies in the Stillness

Beneath the frost, the truth resides,
But so do we, wearing tinted hides.
I'm frozen here, yet feeling warm,
   In icy bliss, I play the charm.

Lies wrapped tight in scarves and hats,
I sidestep truth like cheeky cats.
With frosty breath, I laugh aloud,
As nature sways beneath the cloud.

The snowmen wink with frosty glee,
While I kid myself, unrestrained, free.
In winter's chill, I strive for cheer,
With every giggle, truth disappears.

So let the frostbite mock and tease,
I'll side with laughter in the freeze.
For every flake that falls today,
I'll dance through winter, come what may.

Frosty Breezes of Tranquil Deceit

Breezes blow with frosty cheer,
But warmth within is nowhere near.
I strut and laugh, a brave facade,
While shivering toes betray the charade.

Puffs of smoke swirl, tales of bliss,
Pretending I'm alright, what a hit or miss.
With each cold gust, I play my role,
A jester in winter, ice in my soul.

The sun peeks out, a crafty tease,
As snowflakes dance on the winter breeze.
I sip hot chocolate, a secret drink,
To hide the shivers that make me think.

Yet here we are, with frosty grins,
Faking warmth while the chill begins.
Laugh it off, what a silly game,
In the land of frost, we're all the same.

Caught in a Chilly Web of Truth

Caught in the web of winter's bite,
My nose red as Rudolph's, what a sight!
They say I'm fine, I laugh too loud,
While buried under blankets, I'm part of the crowd.

Hot cocoa spills, I grin and sip,
Pretending my life's a frosty trip.
But ice cubes clink in my mug of cheer,
While frostbite whispers, 'You're not sincere.'

My friends in mittens, they smile so wide,
As we dodge the cold, what a slippery ride!
We dance through snow, in circles we flee,
While secretly wishing for warmth, just me.

It's snowing lies, let's raise a toast,
To the frosty nights we like the most.
With each chilly laugh, truth fades away,
In this winter charade, let's play and stay.

Harmonies of Frost and Silence

In harmony with winters past,
I laugh aloud, but relief won't last.
My cheeks are bright, my breath is fog,
Yet inside I shiver like some lost dog.

Snowflakes fall, a gentle hum,
As laughter bubbles, I'm feeling glum.
They whine about chill, I roll my eyes,
While my teeth chatter, oh what a guise!

Through frosty landscapes, we prance about,
With every slip, I scream and shout.
But the ache in my bones sings a different tune,
While I claim I'm fine, beneath the moon.

We whirl and twirl through the white delight,
As my frozen toes begin the fight.
In this playful frost, a truth held tight,
Behind every smile, hid a frosty plight.

Beneath Every Snowflake, a Whisper

Beneath each snowflake, a secret sigh,
I'm lounging in style, but oh my, my!
Friends say, 'Look at you, brave in the freeze!'
While I'm bundled up tight like warm cozied peas.

They schmooze and prance, all merry and bright,
As I nurse hot soup, to warm my plight.
'Chilly adventures!' they cheer at the door,
But my spirit shivers and yearns for more.

I tell frosty tales with a twist of fate,
While my toes scream loudly, 'We need a break!'
It's a frosty riot wrapped in a grin,
With each biting breeze, I silently spin.

So raise your mugs to the tales we weave,
In this frosty winter, we choose to believe.
Beneath every snowflake, an echo of fun,
As we chill for lies, and the laughter's begun.

Heartbeats in the Frost

In winter's chill, we frolic and play,
Frosty cheeks turn red, what a sight today!
With shivers and giggles, we dance in the breeze,
Hot chocolate awaits as we say 'Oh, please!'

A snowman grins wide with a carrot for a nose,
Holding secrets of warmth in those icy clothes.
We toss snowballs, oh, what a fun fight!
Diving in snow, but oh, what a fright!

Our breath creates clouds that vanish and fade,
While we muse on adventures that winter had made.
Yet underneath layers, the truth could be found,
This chill is a cover, oh, isn't it sound?

We prank each other with ice-cold surprise,
Through laughter and smiles, we dance in disguise.
For warmth is a treasure beneath frosty eaves,
We jest in the cold and the magic it weaves.

A Glassy Smile Beneath Snow

A glassy facade with a shimmery glow,
We chuckle and skip, letting laughter flow.
With snowflakes that tickle, we twirl and we glide,
Beneath the white canvas, our joy cannot hide.

"Oh, what a lovely winter," we cheerfully say,
As icicles dangle and lead us astray.
But beneath the layers of warm, woolen wraps,
Lie hints of a chill and some icy mishaps.

Each snow-covered pathway a slip and a slide,
Yet still we proclaim, "What a glorious ride!"
But giggles and flurries can mask every fall,
For slipping on ice is just part of the ball!

So we build up our castles of frosty delight,
With laughter as armor, we battle the night.
Yet inside our hearts, a little truth sleeps,
Under shattered illusions, warmth quietly creeps.

Frigid Truths in the Warmth of Lies

In cozy campfires, the stories we share,
Of freezing adventures, we giggle and stare.
With marshmallows roasting, the shadows grow long,
Yet whispers reveal that the truth isn't strong.

"Winter's a party!" we all raise a glass,
But frostbite is lurking, waiting to harass.
While we clink our mugs under twinkling lights,
The truth hides away as the coldness ignites.

Snowflakes are falling like feathers from cakes,
"Oh look, how enchanting!" we say with some fakes.
Yet the laughter is real, even if the chill bites,
As we dance 'round the fire, exchanging our sights.

With hats made of wool and boots filled with glee,
We shiver and giggle, all wrapped up for free.
And though we may bicker with snowballing puns,
We can't deny that we're all having fun!

Echoes of a Shivering Soul

Shivers take hold, like a mischievous sprite,
We laugh at the frost while wrapped up so tight.
With scarves all a-twirling and mittens a-fly,
We dash through the snow, oh my, oh my!

Yet echoes of winter hold truths laced with cheek,
Of frigid and funny things we dare not speak.
So we spin 'round in circles, on frozen paths we glide,
While imagining warmth we really can't hide.

As frost kisses noses, we tumble and roll,
In a game of deception that warms up the soul.
Laughter erupts while the chill bites our toes,
But make a mistake, and oh how it goes!

In the echoes of giggles, the chill we outrun,
With every warm story, we gather our fun.
So let winter whisper its secrets so bold,
With hearts ever flickering, we'll brave the cold!

Facade of the Winter Sun

A sunny grin on frosty days,
While my fingers freeze in funny ways.
I dance in snow like a joyful fool,
But inside I'm thawing in a chilly pool.

I sip hot cocoa with a grin so wide,
Yet secretly wishing for a warm, snug ride.
The wispy flakes fall like popcorn surprise,
I pretend to love it while my heart sighs.

Snowman's my buddy, he can't feel the freeze,
I prop him up; he looks like he's pleased.
Yet inside, I know he's falling apart,
Just like my taste for winter's art.

A toasty fire I claim to adore,
But I'm still shivering down to my core.
With layers piled like a marshmallow treat,
I laugh at the frost while I hide my defeat.

Chilled Deceptions Unveiled

I wear a hat like a crown of ice,
With mittens so bright, but oh, what a price!
I trudge through drifts with a feigned delight,
Pretending to thrive in this frigid bite.

The snowflakes dance in a glittery show,
While I watch them fall, oh, how they blow!
Each chilly gust a sarcastic tease,
I chuckle and shiver, oh, winter's unease.

Lemonade thoughts in icicle streams,
I laugh at the frost while they steal my dreams.
The trickling drops from the gutters above,
Are all that remains of my summer love.

So I shovel the walk with a grin so wide,
But lose my footing and come down like a slide.
Still, I play on, for the joy is a ruse,
Warmed by the thoughts of the sun's golden hues.

Frostbitten Facades

I strut like a penguin, full of flair,
With gleaming boots that I like to wear.
Each slip on the ice turns my waltz to a flop,
Yet I giggle along as my layers drop.

The ice crust glimmers with a sparkle so bright,
I tell tales of warmth through the cold winter night.
Swapping hot tea for the frozen air,
I grin as my nose turns a vivid shade rare.

With snowballs in hand, I plot my big scheme,
To launch them at friends and disrupt their daydream.
My laughter rings out like a joyful surprise,
As I stare at the frost through my frosted eyes.

Embracing the chill like a whimsical scene,
I claim I'm the queen of this icy routine.
But when the day ends, and I shiver and sway,
I'd trade my throne for a warm sunny bay.

Mirage of the Frosted Mind

Fluffed-up jackets, I strut in the crowd,
Thinking I'm cool, feeling incredibly proud.
But underneath layers, there's a shiver that lies,
A truth wrapped tightly in hollow disguise.

I chat about snowflakes, their beauty and grace,
While my nose runs free, making me feel out of place.
With laughter I sprinkle like sugar on pies,
Hiding my longing for sunlight that flies.

The winter winds whip, a comical foe,
I stumble and stumble, but I steal the show.
My friends roll their eyes, they've seen this before,
Yet together we spin, slipping out through the door.

As the frosty moon watches, I take one last chance,
To groove with the frost in this silly cold dance.
For deep in my heart, as the cold bites my skin,
I crave warmth and sun in the chaos within.

Beneath Icy Grins

With frosty breath and cheeky grins,
We dance around in winter's spins.
Our toes are numbed, but smiles are wide,
Oh, how we laugh, while truth we hide.

Beneath the snow, a secret's kept,
While icy winds through laughter crept.
We toss snowballs, hit or miss,
In this grand chill, it's pure bliss.

Yet whispers linger, soft but keen,
The warmth we seek is seldom seen.
Wrapped in layers, snug and tight,
We fool ourselves, it's pure delight.

But come the thaw, we'll bare our souls,
And wonder how we lost our goals.
For underneath the frosty game,
Our hearts feel heavy, yet we claim…

a Hearth Lies Buried

Beyond the frost, we take our stand,
Sipping cocoa, with a shaky hand.
We act so tough, like it's all fine,
But inside, we're just a tangled vine.

A flickering flame we try to find,
Beneath this pile of snow, so blind.
With each hot sip, we share a grin,
While freezing hearts are tucked within.

We build snowmen, tall and proud,
While underneath, we're lost in a crowd.
The fire crackles, whispers low,
Yet warmth evades, just like the snow.

In each embrace, we sense the chill,
A hearth of warmth we hope to fill.
But laughter reigns, as icy dreams,
Beneath it all, our humor gleams.

The Illusion of Warmth in Winter's Clutch

In blankets piled, we huddle tight,
Pretending that we're warm and bright.
But every breath meets icy air,
As we trade jokes and silly flair.

With snowflakes dancing on our hats,
We jest about the chill and spats.
Yet fingertips turn numb and blue,
We laugh, yet feel the biting dew.

A snowflake lands upon my nose,
Distinctive tales, as laughter flows.
For warmth's an act, a funny play,
In winter's clutch, we find our way.

For every giggle hides the shiver,
A cozy flame we cease to wither.
The frost may bite, and joy ignite,
In the illusion, we find delight.

Frigid Stars and Silent Whispers

The stars shine bright in winter skies,
But underneath, the truth belies.
With frosty fingers, we wave goodnight,
While shivering hands craft jokes with fright.

Each twinkling light's a frosty tease,
As we share tales of sweet unease.
We wrap ourselves in funny tales,
While our breath hangs thick like frosty gales.

Beneath the laughter, hoarfrost creeps,
As silent whispers fill our sleeps.
We dream of warmth, yet wake to chill,
In this cold maze, we find our thrill.

But oh, the giggles dance like stars,
In bitter cold, we wear no bars.
With every smile, we brave the night,
Frigid moments turn into delight.

Threads of Ice Weaving Deceit

With every snowflake, secrets thread,
As icy whispers fill our head.
We joke of warmth through frozen grins,
While underneath, the laughter thins.

The scarves we wear, they hide the truth,
Of shivers long, that steal our youth.
Yet we parade with gallant glee,
Mocks chill while frost bites playfully.

In snowy forts, we build our walls,
And stage our dramas, since laughter calls.
Yet ice beneath our chuckles lies,
In frigid games where humor flies.

As winter's chill may chill our bones,
Our spirits rise, despite the groans.
For in this freeze, we find our beat,
In threads of ice, we find our heat.

Lies Hidden in the Winter Mist

Snowflakes dance with such glee,
As I sip on my hot tea.
'I'm cozy,' I say with a grin,
While my toes freeze deep within.

Frosty breath like a dragon,
I laugh so hard, it's a braggin'.
But oh, my cheeks are so red,
My wool hat's filled with dread.

Winter's tales of joy do tease,
While the wind whispers, 'Take it, please.'
I wear layers like a sandwich spread,
Yet still complain, 'I'm overfed!'

In this chill, I must insist,
My warmth is too often missed.
So with hot chocolate in sight,
I'll fake that I'm feeling all right!

Echoes of the Chilled Heart.

Outside, the world is all white,
Inside, I'm bundled up tight.
'It's refreshing!' I say with flair,
While my shivers fill the air.

I dance around in my puffy coat,
Turned into a fluffy goat.
My friends are brave, they're out there,
While I snack on chips in a chair.

Ice cream cones in the winter breeze,
They say I'm crazy, I must please.
Yet their laughter, it fuels the fun,
As I sit by the fire, all done.

With frosty breath, I shout cheer,
'Winter is great!' I persevere.
But let the truth rather burn,
Next summer, I really will learn!

Shadows of a Frozen Heart

The snowflakes whisper, 'Don't you freeze!'
Yet I wear multiple layers with ease.
'I'm not cold,' I chuckle away,
While hiding under blankets, I stay.

Mittens stuck to my frosty palms,
I tell myself, 'This has its charms.'
But my fingers and toes have begun to shout,
'Please warm us up! We're not out!'

Frozen toes in fluffy boots,
Jumping jacks just to refute.
I wave my hands like a madman,
While neighbors think I'm part of a plan.

So cheers to the winter's ploy,
I act like a kid with a toy.
In a season that feels like a joke,
I laugh at the ice as I choke!

Whispers Beneath the Ice

Underneath this icy spell,
I spin tales too hard to tell.
'I'm so warm!' I shout with glee,
While my nose looks like a cherry.

Chattering teeth in the chilling air,
But hey, I'm fancy, I'm debonair.
'Outdoor fun is what it's about!'
While I shudder, I scream and shout.

I sip my cocoa, a smirk on my face,
Pretending this season's full of grace.
Yet secretly, I count down the days,
To bask in the sun's warm rays.

So here's to the winter masquerade,
I'll join the jesters in this charade.
With laughter like snowflakes all around,
I'll fake it 'til spring comes back to town!

Hidden Fires Under Layers of Snow

Beneath the frost, a warmth does grow,
A dance of squirrels with stolen dough.
They wear their jackets, oh what a sight,
Furry little thieves in the pale moonlight.

With snowflakes falling, they make their play,
Warming their paws in a humorous way.
They giggle and chatter, oh what a spree,
While I'm bundled up like a wintery burrito, you see!

The snowmen stand tall, but oh can they lie,
With carrot noses and an orange eye.
They claim they're happy, with arms open wide,
But their icicle tears, are hard to hide.

So here's to the snow and its frosty cheer,
In layers we laugh and sip cocoa near.
The chill's just a trick, a facade, a jest,
As I warm my heart in this wintery fest.

Deceptive Offerings from a Winter's Heart

Hot cocoa whispers from a porcelain cup,
Is it a drink or a sipper's hiccup?
The marshmallows float like fluffy lies,
While chocolate dreams brew beneath the skies.

Frosted windows hide giggles and fun,
Much warmer inside when the day is done.
But step outside, you'll find it's a ruse,
As the snowflakes play nothing but a snooze.

The winter sun beams with a mocking grin,
As children slip, land flat on their chin.
They say the ice can't hurt—oh what a joke!
They'll bounce right back, thanks to a friendly poke.

So gather your mittens, and don't shed a tear,
For each icy tumble brings laughter near.
Winter's just playing its comical part,
Deceptive offerings that warm the heart.

Frigid Silhouettes in the Hearth's Glow

By the firelight, shadows dance and glide,
Are those teddy bears or nightly spies?
They tell me stories with their toothy grins,
While I roast marshmallows and tuck my chin.

The frosty windows claim, 'Stay inside!'
Yet kids outside see only the ride.
Fumbling with mittens, they build and they mold,
While their noses turn red—oh, the tales they've told.

Fires crackle with warmth that tickles the toes,
While ice cubes toss in the punch bowl's prose.
They say it's refreshing, but oh my dear friend,
It's just another way to pretend and pretend!

So gather round, toast to winter's grand scheme,
Let the hearth's light kindle our whimsical dream.
Beneath icy exteriors, the laughter flows,
With frigid silhouettes dancing like prose.

Unwinding the Threads of White Lies

Snowflakes come down like little white frauds,
Covering sidewalks with shameless applause.
With every step, a truth goes astray,
As we slip and we trip in a comical ballet.

They lure us outdoors with a smile and a wink,
But frosty fingers are quick to sink.
Yet all of the snowmen are grinning so wide,
Binding their fate in a chilly inside.

Hats on their heads, they strike a pose,
But underneath sneaky sausages lie in rows.
They shout of warmth while they stand so tall,
Yet one good puff brings them packing it all!

So here's to the winter, the giggles, and sighs,
While we untangle the threads of deceitful lies.
For each chilly moment, we laugh in its face,
In this whimsical season, we find our space.